Aisle Survive

HOW TO PLAN YOUR WEDDING
WITHOUT LOSING YOUR MIND

Copyright Page

© 2016 Dee Gaubert

Cover by Wicked Good Book Covers
WickedGoodBookCovers.com

Photo by Shani Barel

Print Interior Design by Colleen Sheehan
WDRBookDesign.com

Aisle Survive

HOW TO PLAN YOUR WEDDING
WITHOUT LOSING YOUR MIND

DEE GAUBERT

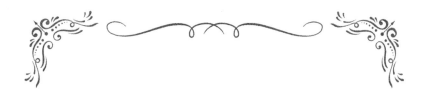

Introduction

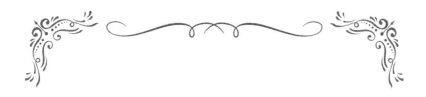

If you're reading this, you're probably a bride or groom. I invite you right now to put this book down and google this: "Old wedding photos." You'll see pretty basic photos of the bride and groom, the bride holding a bouquet, and both smiling and staring at the camera. Even celebrity photos of the biggest stars of the day show the bride and groom simply dressed in smart outfits, perhaps cutting some cake after a quick ceremony.

Now go back to your Pinterest board, or your favorite wedding blog. The photos are a lot different, aren't they? Loving closeups of bouquets, carefully posed photos of bride and groom gazing into each other's eyes; bridal party members in matching robes, personally mono-gramed; shot after shot after shot of décor: Bar signage, centerpieces, that favor of hand-mixed spices inspired from that perfect seafood dish they had on that trip to Hawaii when he pro-posed, etc. etc. etc. Weddings aren't just a sen-timental milestone any more. They're an elite sport, a high-end competition: who has the most beautiful, most finely detailed celebration - and who can do it with the lowest budget? Who can be...perfect? And for most couples, it's not necessarily a competition with other brides and grooms, but with themselves. That high bar, set internally, is one they constantly try to reach.

With the onset of the internet, digital photography, and wedding-obsessed blogs, couples are inundated with millions of internet photos of the "perfect" wedding. And these weddings aren't necessarily celebrity weddings – in fact, I daresay many Average Joe and Jane's weddings outshine many celebrity weddings, these days. (Celebrities don't really have anything to prove to anyone – they often keep it pretty simple.) Photos of décor show clever ideas, reusing everyday objects and over-scaling the simplest of elements. For example, where one plate would do, a bride and groom can add a charger underneath; a salad plate on top; a folded napkin tied across; and a jeweled brooch in the middle. The guests sit down and have no idea what to do with all of this, and try to make do as best they can, and the caterers rush to clear all the plates (which they cannot, per health code, re-use) and still serve the first course in a timely fashion. At the end of the night, brooches are on the floor, encrusted with food, or stomped on the floor by a waiter, and the client is out a few extra hundred bucks for all those plates.

Creating the perfect night exacts a lot of pressure on brides and grooms, especially when their families weigh in, and everyone's trying to stay on a budget. As a wedding planner for years now, I have witnessed couples and their families overthinking the very basic elements of the wedding; spending hours mulling over the absolute right mix of flowers for their centerpieces, agonize over the exact pattern for their lighting, or freak out over some construction at the hotel parking garage on the whole other side of the property that not even their guests are going to know about. Time-intensive debates about the tiniest of details became the norm.

Meantime, I continued to build my corporate event business – launch parties, book signings, retreats, and such. Some of the clients barely had time to talk to me, as they were busy with their day-to-day work – they give quick approvals, and very little debate when making a decision. Emotions rarely got in the way, and they had sensible time frames given that they had to reach some objectives on a deadline and get the job done. I realized, as a corporate planner,

I was working better hours and with less stress and exhaustion. It was a hard choice, but I had to delegate the majority of my weddings to my team of associates, and I personally took over the corporate events. While I oversee my associates' weddings with glee and enthusiasm, I personally am not running them except for a very few.

Just so you know, I was a bride too, so I know what it's like to go down the rabbit hole. During the planning process, I was legitimately stressed. We were worried about people we couldn't invite, and if they'd still be our friends after they found out they weren't on the list. And we were worried about the ones we could invite: What if more people showed up than expected? While my parents generously paid for the venue, food, and beverage, we were constantly nervous about expenses for the rest of the event. We had to invite 40 additional important family members who lived overseas, and panicked that they would all come – and blow our budget (and my parents' generous gift). And lastly, I was just annoyed that there was so much work involved.

So, I did the bare minimum of work. I'm not kidding. I know, I'm a wedding planner – and I took the easy way out for my own shindig? But I did! At that time, I had a busy job as a television producer and simply was too lazy, honestly, to spend my hard-earned free time putting any more effort into the big day than was necessary. Also, the dynamics of the guest list was emotionally exhausting, and I kind of lost my mind a little bit. I found myself indulging in an odd habit: Making gin and tonics and watching 1930s pirate movies. If that's not a sign you've gone off the deep end, I have no idea what is. (PS: I highly recommend Errol Flynn's 1940 classic, The Sea Hawk!)

And if I did it all again? I'd change a couple things – I'd invest in nicer chairs and some uplighting for the reception; and I'd spend a little more on my reception dress. Everything else, I wouldn't change a bit. And yes, that's after executing gorgeous, big, amazing weddings where everything from the napkin tie to the lighting was executed to perfection. Why? Because I'm just thrilled my husband and I are delighted to be in each other's company ten years later. We have an amazing marriage, and nothing we did that night to make our reception more beautiful would have changed that.

That's why I'm writing is this book: To invite couples to engage in what really matters – the emotion of the day, and the meaning behind it.

This isn't a book aimed at bridezillas or Type-A grooms - I'm talking about sane, kind human beings who will obsess and hand-wring about small details about their wedding as if they, too, have gone down the wedding rabbit hole, like me – but instead of escaping to Errol Flynn swinging on a rope and saving a ship, they stay down the hole and walk around in circles over and over again trying to decide if seeded – or non seeded?? – eucalyptus is EXACTLY the right greenery to use in their centerpieces? It's a plea for couples to stop torturing themselves (and, I hate to say it, their loved ones and the vendors they've hired as well) when there is so little reward in the agonizing.

I'm brutally honest in this book, but it all comes from a place of compassion. I know first-hand that your wedding is a singular, special day, and I never want to see someone look back and resent the planning process. After reading this book, you will hopefully have a sense of relief, and tools for processing the various decisions you have to make, with a sense of sanity, security, and a laugh or two.

We'll focus on three things that cause the most fretting: Design, budget, and family.

First, we'll zoom out for a little perspective.

One

FIRST WORLD PROBLEMS

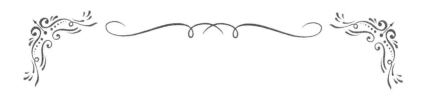

The importance of your wedding, in relation to other world issues:

1. ISIS and Middle East Unrest
2. Post-recession economy
3. Syrian Refugee Crisis
4. Russia and Ukrainian conflict
5. North Korea Nuclear Testing
6. World hunger
7. Struggling public schools
8. Heroin epidemic
9. High school dropout rate
10. Teen pregnancy
11. Pollution
12. Bad Traffic
13. Will Khloe Kardashian ever find true love?
14. Cellulite: Still around, still no cure
15. Trader Joe's discontinued my favorite snack
16. Your wedding.

I remember working with a bride on her floral décor for her ceremony. The vision had changed once or twice; in her attempt to discuss it, she started to almost panic. I watched her sit back and fall silent, almost catatonic, uncertain what to do. We had already talked about a really great idea and agreed to a few inspiration photos. What was the issue, and why was it so important? We weren't brokering the Iran nuclear deal here, people. This was a wedding.

Over time, and a few hours (and hours...and hours) of back and forth, we finally locked in on a few cohesive ideas. But this bride, I still wonder why she was so intense about getting the flowers just right, when what we had originally devised was so very lovely and on-theme.

I struggled to find perspective in my own wedding planning, and what helped was to let go. I remember the week of the wedding; my catering sales manager left without any notice to her work place (my venue was a vintage ocean liner permanently docked in Southern California). There was confusion with the person who took over, as in, they thought my ceremony started three hours later than agreed to (!), and it really freaked me out. Then, I had a new coworker come on board the very week of my wedding, and had to hurriedly hand off my work to her, so I could leave for my honeymoon - but I had only 1.5 days off that week, which was absolute lunacy, by the way. I was not in a good place.

I took a moment as I was packing for the weekend and honeymoon, and I told myself this: You are going to go to your bachelorette party. You are going to have fun. You are going to have fun the rest of the weekend and enjoy every single minute. And even if the ship sinks during the wedding, you're going to go down laughing and sipping champagne. This day, this experience, this weekend, will never happen again. You've done all you can to make sure it's going to be amazing. You will now sit back, and take it all in.

And guess what; I did enjoy it, every single minute of it. I took deep breaths during the ceremony and stared into my husband's eyes, and still remember how he was looking at me. (By the way, the cue to walk down the aisle never got to him, so he wasn't standing at the altar when I got there, which I still think is hilarious. Life is full of funny accidents – your wedding may have a couple, too.) I recall side conversations with dear friends throughout the reception. I recall how much fun my parents had with their family and friends; it had been so long since they were all in the same place. Some of them are gone now; I treasure these memories. I met a family related to my husband who flew all the way from Chile, and loved hearing about their lives back home. It was awesome. And thank goodness I had a coordinator take over the reins and oversee the wedding so I could kick back and truly relax the day of my event.

In the planning process, there are things that don't always work out. What you have to remember is this: It's about an experience. It's about ephemeral moments that could go away that you have to grasp onto and treasure. The hours you spent finding just the right glass votives has nothing to do with the 10 minute catch up you have with your second cousin that you haven't seen in 20 years. Like, literally nothing. Give your décor and the details their fair shake; but don't dwell, if the flower you want isn't in season or the DJ you wanted so desperately is already booked. Let it go, because you need to be open for positive energy and love that you will be soaking in on the big day.

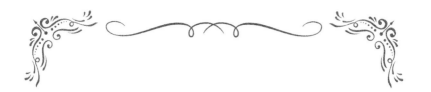

Two

THE DEVIL IN DESIGN

Based on my experience, the main element of weddings that drives most couples crazy is design. Weddings have now become showcases for good taste. Couples try to get their weddings published. They become consumed with clicking on thousands of images online.

The main issue I've found is indecision. With too many choices, with thousands of possibilities popping up after entering in a few keywords, how do you decide on your bouquet, centerpieces, favors? I sympathize with couples these days – it's overwhelming. But, it's gotten to the point where I've warned my clients that if they change their design one more time, there's hell to pay – "if you send another tabletop décor idea six weeks before the wedding, I'm going to be very mad!" It's in good fun...but they know I mean it! Vendors can't constantly change on a whim – it takes time to draft new proposals, revise design boards, research new items, which may mean more fees to pay, too. And what you're doing...well, it's not really accomplishing anything. You're playing a shell game: exchanging one gorgeous look for another.

Most of all, your guests really don't care what the wedding looks like. I'm sorry, guys, but it's true. More than fair for YOU to care, but ultimately it's a waste of time to belabor an already lovely idea to make it somehow... more lovely? Switching blush dahlias for ivory ones isn't going to make a big impact.

The feedback I get from my clients after their wedding is done, is almost verbatim, as follows: "Everyone had so much fun." "It was a blast." "Our guests had an amazing time." I have never heard, "Our guests loved every minute, and they really appreciated that we chose garden roses over the standard because they knew the standard roses would have been a disaster." Sure, we've heard from guests how generally beautiful the wedding is, but it's more the big picture that makes the most impact.

Recently, I was assisting a colleague who gifted her coordination services to a family friend. The bride's family pulled up with three cars worth of décor. We weren't warned, and were absolutely frantic. Where one or two framed quotes would work, there were 15; where the natural backdrop of the space would work, there were handmade pieces of furniture not needed for their intimate, small guest count. As soon as we implemented the design, we had to start tearing it all down. We needed at least two more hands to help but we had to barrel through and start discreetly packing up décor earlier in the process than we typically would have needed to. (Otherwise, we would have stayed so late that the venue would have charged the clients overtime.) I started thinking: Is this a catalog shoot, or a wedding?

A good designer knows when to stop. If you are not a designer or work in visual conceptualization on a regular basis, and keep questioning and changing your look constantly, the reason you may sense frustration with your professional design vendors is because they knew you should have stopped messing with the look about two changes ago. I have corporate clients that need design conceptualization and full production in about a month's time. We make a few tweaks here and there, then we're done. We need everything to look spot-on, especially if it's a product launch where attendees are going to actively post on Instagram photos of the event. Every time, because of our design presentation, we've had excellent social media engagement from the event. So trust me, if you have a professional designer, planner, and florist telling you your look is great, it's great. Messing with it doesn't really enhance anything.

Sometimes brides and grooms mimic a look they saw online in order to go with a low-risk endeavor, versus coming up with a fun, brand new look that's all their own. It's more important to have a cohesive design that has your fingerprints on it, versus copying something just to try to impress your guests. That said, if you are going bonkers with indecision, feel free to pick a basic imprint of an existing design and tweak a few things to make it your own. Just don't copy a stationary design or other very unique decorative piece, without paying the original vendor to recreate it.

Often, a florist or designer will brainstorm with a client about the overall design, and start suggesting ideas and concepts. The client will furrow their brow and then say, "I just can't visualize it." The answer to that is, "perhaps you can't, but we can. So the question is, do you trust us to visualize it for you?" It's almost like going to an accountant, a doctor, or a mechanic. I can't visualize what timing belt or doohickey the mechanic is talking about, but I trust he's going to fix it. Think of those old wedding photos: Can you imagine the couples being concerned about their bouquets? Back then, people perhaps only had one or two inspiration photos from magazines or books to show their vendors. They gave the florist a few ideas and then voila, they had a bouquet. Done. Again, clients are starting to think their décor needs to compete with a magazine shoot or catalog presentation, but it's a live event about emotions and sentiment, not to sell items or dazzle a national readership.

Here are my tips to cut through the overwhelm of the world wide web and focus your vision:

1. Think about what your style is. Is it chic and modern? Homey and vintage? Pop art? Only search online for inspiration related to that aesthetic. Do not, repeat, do not get distracted once you set your theme, and makes sure it aligns with your venue. If you chose a vintage art-deco space, don't go with farm-rustic décor.

2. Let your budget make decisions. Sometimes we've had to nix an idea due to budget, so we come up with something different, cool, and totally unique.

3. Trust your vendors. If you want to try to combine a few looks that your florist says isn't a good idea, allow them to come up with a compromise and unless it's totally off-theme (in which case, the florist is probably not the right fit), go with it. It's their work; they want to show well, too.

4. The issue coordinators and planners constantly run into is clients demanding absolute perfection of dozens of details on a very busy day – your wedding day. Some wedding inspiration photos that are popular online are of styled shoots, where vendors come together and belabor for hours to tweak the look "just so." On a wedding day, the vendors don't have time for it. And if you have only a couple hours in the space prior to the ceremony, it's very difficult to execute a complicated look.

5. Don't go overboard with setup. We've had clients insist on bringing their own décor and instead of hiring more of my team, they'll execute the setup themselves. We'll assist as best we can, of course, but the family always ends up stressed. I tend to look around see waaaay too much stuff. Too many design elements become repetitive and lose their impact. My tip: Pack no more than a car trunk's worth of décor.

Three

PARENTAL UNITS

I keep finding myself emailing my mom, thanking her and my dad for not constantly interfering with our wedding planning, even though they paid for a very large portion of it. My mom's reaction is incredulous. I'm paraphrasing, but basically her response is: "We raised you to be a responsible adult. Why wouldn't I trust you to plan the wedding?"

Most times, working with a set of parents along with the bride and groom is a fairly easy, smooth process. Occasionally, though, a whole phalanx of family will attend a meeting. I've got to run by ideas for approval by 3-4 people sometimes. I'm not talking about having a few sidebar conversations with parents here and there to work out a few issues, get approvals for one or two expenses–the family members are instead overtaking the planning process and constantly throwing in their two cents even when the bride or groom have a perfectly acceptable idea, and are doing so with all due respect to their parents. I've witnessed arguments over tiny, inconsequential things, that have been very unpleasant to sit through and weren't necessary to broker an agreement.

Certainly I've worked with parents who worked with me solely because their child is busy and wants their parent to be their agent, so to speak; or were involved because they were great with logistics and it was a reasonable, non-dramatic group effort - happens all the time. But lately, for every easy planning process, there have been others worthy of soap opera drama.

But, it takes two to tango. If you're a couple, and one or more parents are overly exerting their influence, try to step back and see if it's as big a deal as it seems. If they're paying for most of it, requests like approving the final center-piece design, overseeing their side of the family's seating chart, and giving their blessing on the final menu – with a normal amount of polite discussion – is totally fair. Remember, these are the people who raised you from a wee little boy or girl, and are going through a really intense amount of emotions – as well as possibly a significant financial sacrifice.

That said, if they are taking over the process to the point where they are shutting you out of meetings, talking to vendors as if it's their wedding and not yours, and provoking raised-voice arguments (and again, be honest that you yourself are not being the unreasonable one) - it's important to consider cutting the cord. If you're old enough to get married, you're old enough to pay for the majority of your wedding, if that's what it takes. Meet with them or schedule a phone call, and simply state that you are going to make the majority of decisions within a few frameworks: 1. Ensure the guests they want to invite are invited. 2. Ensure they are happy with the final menu. 3. Allow them to weigh in on the seating chart so they can seat their closest friends and family around them. From there, if they still want to interfere, consider paying for the entire wedding yourself or postpone it till you can afford it.

If you are a parent that has found you are getting into arguments every step of the way with your child, be sure to take a step back and ask yourself how important it is to have total control. If your child wants to wear a Game of Thrones outfit and play goth music all night, okay, I get it, you have a right to be a little taken aback. If your child is planning a fairly traditional affair, have a powwow about general budget and spending expectations, talk guest count and general parameters - then get comfortable with those guidelines and work within them, and try to calmly and objectively discuss any further issues or disagreements. This will cost you less time and energy and ensure a smoother process.

The best examples I've seen of parental involvement? A mom and daughter collaborating on design and building a few DIY projects for décor; a dad helping create a song list for cocktail hour; a mother who is handling most of the planning on her son's behalf because he and his fiancée live out of town, and dutifully creating the event based on their tastes and wishes.

Those parents get gold stars for being supportive, loving, and creative – speeding the process along, instead of adding hurdles every step of the way.

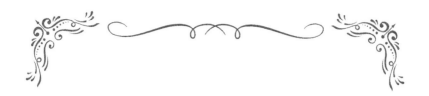

Four

REAL WORLD BUDGETING

The statistics say the average wedding is about $30,000, but in major metropolitan areas, it's hard to get by for less $45-50k. Many times I'll chat with a potential client that wants to have a wedding for $15,000 total. And you know what, I wish that were the case. It's absurd how much these events cost.

There's a topsy-turvy feel in our economy now, where people's wages don't stretch as far as they use to. Experts say that you could buy the same amount of goods with today's average hourly wage as you could in 1979. That's almost 40 years ago! We're making more, but can't afford more. We now rely on buying things from overseas where living standards are low, and thus, so are hourly wages, so we buy these material goods cheaply. However, our own rent, gas, and other homegrown costs of living are high.

The services and many goods you source for your wedding are all local, such as food and labor, so your vendors have to charge proportionally higher for their services compared to how cheaply you got your, say, wedding favors made in China.

Before you do a thing – I mean sign any vendor, venue, anything – please secure a budget evaluation from a wedding professional or talk frankly with a friend who has already had their wedding, with a similar venue and guest count. It's so eye opening, and allows you to make changes in your expectations and avoid huge, stressful surprises down the road. Some of my clients who have asked for a budget consult have postponed their wedding till they saved more cash, and in the long run, it saved them so much money and anxiety. Yet, the cost of hiring a budget consultant is a tiny fraction of the overall wedding costs.

Once you know your budget, get cozy with it. I've parted ways with clients that, as I called it, "spoke out of both sides of their mouths." They want to pay very little for alcohol, but absolutely HAD to have the Veuve Cliquot poured for champagne toast. Or want a cinematic masterpiece for their wedding video and don't expect to pay more than $1,000. I can't make numbers up; I wish I could, but my magic wand has not arrived yet from Hogwart's. So, embrace the reality of your numbers, and work within that total bottom line. Keep things simple, which in the long run will inform your planning process with a lower-stress, easygoing feel.

As far as vendor pricing, beware of the 'too good to be true' price. As a small business owner in the world of events, working in a large metropolitan area, I know instinctively how much a vendor needs to make in order to earn a living, and which ones are worth paying a premium. My clients and I evaluate a realistic budget before making the first move in signing a venue, a photographer, and so on. There is a natural edge – if I see a vendor charging well below-market, I know something's up. And I have observed 9 out of 10 times (well, that's an estimate – but I know it's close to accurate!) the "cheaper-than-everyone-else vendor" is a problem. They leave damage to the property, show up late, act unprofessionally. I can almost set my watch to it. And who has to overcompensate in order to ensure a smooth wedding? Me, the DJ, photographer, whoever else on the team knows how to run a smooth, efficient wedding. Unfortunately clients sometimes pay the price, too. So beware the 'good deal' and be sure to get a rock solid contract from all of your vendors.

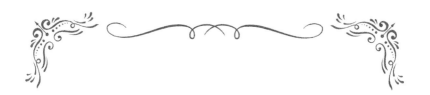

In Summary

GO FORTH AND ENJOY YOUR SANITY!

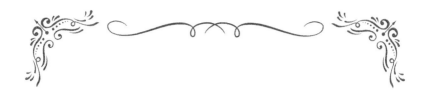

Now that you've read about the reality behind the 'perfection' of weddings, I hope you give yourself permission to really absorb the joy and emotion beyond the day; to diplomatically deflect family issues; and most of all, to shed any pressure you feel to have the very most beautiful-est prettiest, Instagrammable-ist wedding ever. If you know you are marrying the best person in the world for you, you don't have anything to prove. Breathe deeply through the stressful moments, and don't create any more by delving too deep in minutae. I wish you joy and happiness in your wedding day, and in your life together. Happy planning!

For more advice, visit

WWW.AISLESURVIVE.COM

About the Author

Dee Gaubert is the founder of No Worries Event Planning. As a premier wedding planner and designer, she has planned Weddings and events in Los Angeles and abroad, including several in Paris, France. Her events have been featured in such publications as People Magazine, Us Weekly, and Martha Stewart Weddings. While she does have celebrity clientele, every couple is a celebrity in her eyes and she treats each one with compassion and a playful sense of humor. Dee lives in Encino, California, with her husband, son, and their other "kids" — two dogs and a cat.

AISLE SURVIVE